What Happened at the Boston Massacre?

US History Lessons for Kids 6th Grade

Children's American History

BABY PROFESSOR
EDUCATION KIDS

Speedy Publishing LLC

40 E. Main St. #1156

Newark, DE 19711

www.speedypublishing.com

Copyright 2017

All Rights reserved. No part of this book may be reproduced or used in any way or form or by any means whether electronic or mechanical, this means that you cannot record or photocopy any material ideas or tips that are provided in this book

The Boston Massacre took place on March 5, 1770 in a midnight raid when British soldiers in Boston opened fire on some American colonists causing five men to die. Read further to learn more about it, why it happened and how it ended.

TOWNSHEND ACTS

Before the Boston Massacre, the British created many additional taxes on American Colonies which included taxes on glass, tea, lead, paint and paper. These came to be known as Townshend Acts. These laws were not received well by the colonies. The colonies then began to protest similar to what they did when Britain levied the Stamp Act and they brought soldiers in to maintain order. They received their name as they were introduced by Charles Townshend of the British Parliament. These Acts continued to drive the American colonists towards a revolution. They disclosed that the British did not comprehend that "taxation without representation" really was a big deal to most of the colonists.

CHARLES TOWNSHEND

These laws added taxes and took away freedoms. Taxes were placed on imported paint, paper, tea, glass and lead as well to establishing the American Customs Board to receive these taxes. It also gave them the right to create new courts to indict smugglers without the use of a jury. British officials were given the right to search businesses and houses. The Townshend Acts were created to pay the salaries of judges, governors and other officials.

They felt the colonists would go along with these taxes. They repealed the Stamp Act due to protests, but thought that the import taxes were okay. However, they were wrong, and the colonists again protested against the taxes.

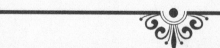

The colonies did not have permission to have representation in the Parliament.

They thought this unconstitutional. It was more about principle than the tax cost.

CONSEQUENCES

This caused unrest with the colonies. Letters from a Farmer in Pennsylvania, were essays against these acts written by John Dickinson. He later wrote the Articles of the Confederation. He wrote that there would be more taxes forthcoming if they continued to pay them. Soon the merchants started boycotting British merchandise. They then started smuggling merchandise in order to avoid these taxes. The British panicked when the protests became violent and people were killed. This became to be known as the Boston Massacre.

JOHN DICKINSON

King Street, Boston

THE BOSTON MASSACRE

On March 5, 1770, it began in the evening starting with an argument between a few colonists and British Private White outside of the Custom House located on King Street in Boston. It got worse as additional colonists congregated and started harassing Private White.

The group of colonists grew to more than 50. Captain Thomas Preston, a British officer, sent several soldiers to the Custom House to see if they could get things under control. Unfortunately, once the crowd saw the British soldiers with bayonets, things got worse. They started shouting at the soldiers and challenging them to fire at them.

British Soldiers

Captain Preston showed up in an effort to break up the crowd. An object was then thrown from someone in the crowd striking Private Montgomery knocking him down. He then decided to fire his weapon. This was followed by several other soldiers firing their weapons. Three colonists were killed immediately with two later ended up dying from their wounds.

AFTER THE MASSACRE

Thomas Hutchinson, Boston's acting governor, was eventually able to get the crowd dispersed. Thirteen arrests were made which consisted of eight of Britain's soldiers, four civilians and one officer. They were taken to jail facing murder charges. The city then removed the British troops.

THOMAS HUTCHINSON

JOHN ADAMS

THE TRIALS

On November 27, 1770, the trials of eight soldiers started. The government wished them a fair trial, but experienced problems getting legal representation for them. John Adams finally agreed to represent them. Even as a patriot, John Adams felt that they should have a trial that was fair. He argued that they had the right to defend themselves. He said that they felt the crowd was dangerous. While two soldiers were found guilty of manslaughter, six were found to be not guilty.

CONSEQUENCES

The massacre came to be known as a cry for patriotism. The Sons of Liberty and similar groups used it to show the tribulations of the rules of the British. While the American Revolution did not begin for five more years, it certainly motivated people to see British rule in a whole new way.

GENERAL THE HON. THOS. GAGE
1768

THOMAS GAGE

THE INTOLERABLE ACTS

In retribution, the British approved the Coercive Acts, known by the colonists as the Intolerable Acts. Soldiers would block the trade in and out of Boston. The port was then closed until the tea was paid for and town meetings were banned. General Thomas Gage was then made the governor and took control.

These Acts consisted of five separate laws and were passed in 1774 against the American Colonies by British Parliament. The name stemmed from American Patriots that thought they could no longer "tolerate" such biased laws.

These five were passed by the British as punishment.

- ↳ Boston Port Act
- ↳ Massachusetts Government Act
- ↳ Administration of Justice Act
- ↳ Quartering Act
- ↳ Quebec Act

BOSTON PORT ACT

This Act became the first of the Acts that were passed. It was passed as punishment of Boston as a result of the Boston Tea Party. The port was closed to all ships until the tea that they dumped in the water was paid for. Many thought the punishment unfair since it punished all citizens for the crime committed by a few. Supplies were then sent to Boston by other American Colonies.

Old State House. Boston Massachusetts

MASSACHUSETTS GOVERNMENT ACT

The act that changed the Massachusetts government was known as the Massachusetts Government Act. The governor was provided with more power and power was taken from the colonies. Many government officials previously elected by the citizens now would be named by their governor. This angered all of the Massachusetts colonies and the other colonies became fearful. If they could do this in Boston, they might do the same to the remaining colonies.

ADMINISTRATION OF JUSTICE ACT

The Administration of Justice act permitted the governor to move trials against officials to Great Britain. The colonies thought this provide too much protection for these officials. Witnesses had to travel to Britain to testify against a government official, which made is almost impossible to get a conviction. It then became known as the "Murder Act" since they felt it would provide officials with the ability to get away with murder.

QUARTERING ACT

The Quartering Act of 1765 became the Quartering Act of 1774, expanding on the original Act. This stated that colonies were required to provide sleeping quarters for the British. If they were not available, they could stay in hotels, barns and homes.

QUEBEC ACT

This Act expanded British Canadian territory to the Ohio Valley. The Quebec Province was then made a Catholic province. While this act was not a direct result of the Boston Tea Party, it passed along with the other acts. This act also made the American colonists angry. They did not like losing their Ohio land or being close to a Catholic province.

Quebec Province

RESULTING EFFECTS OF THESE ACTS

The American patriots thought they took away part of their freedom, which then actually helped the colonies to unite and they became closer to a revolution.

DID YOU KNOW?

The British labeled the Massacre as the "Incident on King Street". After it took place, both sides attempted to utilize newspaper propaganda to make the others look bad.

King Street

The Custom Hall was labeled as "Butcher's Hall" in an infamous engraving by Paul Revere showing Captain Preston giving orders to his men to fire (which he did not do).

Some evidence indicates that the colonies planned the attack of the soldiers.

CRISPUS ATTUCKS

Crispus Attucks, a slave that had runaway to be a sailor, was killed. Samuel Gray, Patrick Carr, Samuel Maverick, and James Caldwell were killed. The four civilians that were arrested were found not guilty due to the lack of evidence against them.

Sons of Liberty formed after the massacre and consisted of at least 80 chapters around Massachusetts.

ſt—p! ſt—p! No:

ng, December 17, 1765.

rue-born Sons of Li-

deſired to meet under LIBERTY-
Clock, THIS DAY, to hear the
gnation, under Oath, of ANDREW
ſtributor of Stamps for the Province
ëtts-Bay.

Reſignation ? YES.

SAMUEL ADAMS

Writing about ideas and news, the Committees of Correspondence was summoned by Samuel Adams, often referred to as "Firebrand of the American Revolution". They helped unite the colonies in order to obtain their freedom.

Passing in 1773, what became known as the British Tea Act, regulated that the colonists were only permitted to purchase tea from the East Indian Company. The plan was to assist the company in selling cheaper to the Americans, which in turn, undercut prices charged by local merchants in the colonies.

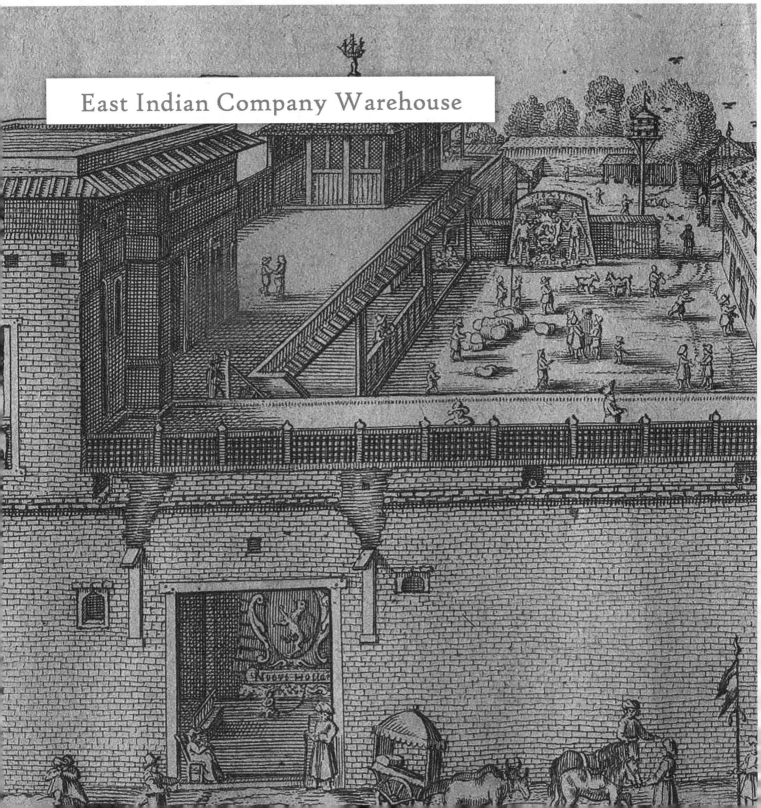

East Indian Company Warehouse

Old South Church

More than 5,000 Bostonians met on December 16, at the Old South Church to object to this Act. They dressed like Indians and went to the ships in the Harbor and dumped 45 tons of tea into the water.

To find out more about the Boston Massacre, as well as the events leading up to it, go to your local library, research the internet, and ask questions of your teachers, family and friends.

Visit

BABY PROFESSOR
EDUCATION KIDS

www.BabyProfessorBooks.com

to download Free Baby Professor eBooks
and view our catalog of new and exciting
Children's Books

CPSIA information can be obtained
at www.ICGtesting.com
Printed in the USA
LVHW061621300719
625868LV00017B/79/P

9 781541 912908